The Phoenix Strategy: How Great Companies Reinvent Themselves to Dominate New Markets

by David Klein

Table of Contents

Introduction: The Anatomy of a Successful Business Pivot

Part I: The Early Pioneers

Chapter 1: From Paper to Technology - How Nintendo's Playing Card Business Became a Gaming Empire

Chapter 2: Western Union's Evolution: From Telegraph Pioneer to Global Financial Services

Chapter 3: Nokia's Journey: From Rubber Boots to Mobile Telecommunications

Part II: Crisis-Driven Transformations

Chapter 4: IBM's Strategic Shift: From Hardware Giant to Services Leader

Chapter 5: Marvel Entertainment: From Bankruptcy to Entertainment Powerhouse

Chapter 6: Netflix: The Strategic Evolution from DVD Rentals to Streaming Giant

Chapter 7: Fujifilm's Digital Response: Why It Succeeded Where Kodak Failed

Part III: Market Opportunity Pivots

Chapter 8: Amazon: From Online Bookstore to Everything Store and Cloud Computing Leader

Chapter 9: Microsoft's Cloud Revolution: Redefining Success in the Post-PC Era

Chapter 10: Adobe: The Brilliant Shift from Boxed Software to Cloud Subscriptions

Conclusion: Lessons from History's Greatest Business Transformations

Introduction: The Anatomy of a Successful Business Pivot

In the unforgiving landscape of global commerce, survival often demands more than mere adaptation—it requires complete reinvention. The ability to pivot, to fundamentally transform a business model while maintaining organizational coherence, has become the defining characteristic of enduring enterprises. This transformation is not merely about changing direction; it is about recognizing the precise moment when the current path becomes unsustainable and having the courage to chart a new course.

Throughout history, some of the world's most successful companies have undergone dramatic transformations that would have been unimaginable to their founders. Nintendo, a company that began by manufacturing playing cards in 1889, now dominates the video game industry. IBM, once synonymous with personal computers, has reinvented itself as a cloud computing and artificial intelligence pioneer. These transformations represent more than mere product line extensions—they embody fundamental shifts in organizational DNA.

The anatomy of a successful pivot comprises three critical elements: timing, execution, and vision. Timing requires an almost prescient ability to recognize market shifts before they become obvious to competitors. Execution demands the operational excellence to maintain current business operations while building new capabilities. Vision necessitates the courage to imagine a future that may seem disconnected from the company's historical identity.

In this book, we will dissect some of the most significant business pivots in corporate history, examining both successes and failures to distill actionable insights for modern business leaders. Through extensive research and analysis, we will explore how companies across different sectors and eras have managed to reinvent themselves successfully—and why others failed in their attempts.

Our journey through corporate transformation is organized into six distinct parts, each illuminating different aspects of the pivoting phenomenon:

Part I: The Early Pioneers examines the foundational cases of corporate transformation, including Nintendo's evolution from playing cards to video games and Nokia's remarkable journey from rubber boots to mobile telecommunications. These cases demonstrate that successful pivots have been possible throughout business history, not just in the digital age.

Part II: Crisis-Driven Transformations explores how companies like Marvel Entertainment and Netflix turned potential disaster into opportunity through strategic reinvention. These stories reveal how existential threats can catalyze innovative thinking and bold action.

Part III: Market Opportunity Pivots analyzes companies like Amazon and Microsoft, which underwent transformations not from necessity but from recognizing and seizing emerging opportunities. Their stories illustrate how proactive pivots can be even more powerful than reactive ones.

The business pivot is not merely a defensive maneuver to avoid obsolescence; it is increasingly becoming an offensive strategy to create new value and capture emerging opportunities. As we move deeper into an era of unprecedented technological change and market disruption, the ability to pivot effectively may well become the most crucial capability for organizational survival and success.

This book serves as both a historical record of remarkable corporate transformations and a practical guide for leaders contemplating their own pivots. Through these pages, we will explore not just the what and how of successful pivots, but also the why— the strategic reasoning and market insights that drove these transformational decisions.

The lessons contained within these chapters are not merely academic; they are vital insights for any organization facing the prospect of fundamental change. As we will see, the most successful pivots are not random acts of desperation but carefully orchestrated transformations that balance risk and opportunity, tradition and innovation, stability and change.

Let us begin our exploration of how great companies reinvent themselves, and in doing so, write new chapters in the history of business innovation and transformation.

Chapter 1: From Paper to Technology - How Nintendo's Playing Card Business Became a Gaming Empire

In the bustling streets of Kyoto in 1889, Fusajiro Yamauchi opened a modest shop called "Nintendo Koppai," specializing in handmade playing cards for traditional Japanese card games. Little did he know that this humble beginning would evolve into one of the most influential technology companies in the world. Nintendo's transformation from a playing card manufacturer to a global gaming powerhouse represents one of the most remarkable pivots in business history, demonstrating how deeply rooted traditional companies can successfully reinvent themselves in the face of changing markets and technological innovation.

Origins in Traditional Gaming

Nintendo's initial business model centered around the production of hanafuda cards, traditional Japanese playing cards used in various games. The company had carved out a respectable niche in Japan's gaming culture, with their handcrafted cards becoming known for their quality and artistry. By the 1950s, under the leadership of Hiroshi Yamauchi, the founder's grandson, Nintendo had established itself as Japan's leading playing card manufacturer. The company's market position was strong but ultimately limited by the inherent constraints of the traditional gaming market.

In 1959, Nintendo took its first step toward diversification by partnering with Disney to produce playing cards featuring Disney characters. This strategic move expanded their market reach and demonstrated early signs of the company's ability to recognize the value of character-driven entertainment. However, this success would soon be challenged by fundamental shifts in Japanese society and global entertainment trends.

Catalysts for Change

The 1960s brought significant challenges to Nintendo's traditional business model. The playing card market was reaching saturation, and changing leisure patterns in Japanese society meant that traditional card games were losing their cultural prominence. The company's revenue from playing cards began to plateau, and Yamauchi recognized that relying solely on this traditional market would eventually lead to stagnation or decline.

Moreover, the rise of television and electronic entertainment was beginning to transform how people spent their leisure time. This technological shift presented both a threat to traditional gaming and an opportunity for companies willing to embrace new forms of entertainment. The catalyst for Nintendo's pivot wasn't a single moment of crisis but rather a gradual recognition that the future of gaming would be fundamentally different from its past.

Strategic Decision-Making and Key Players

Hiroshi Yamauchi emerged as the architect of Nintendo's transformation. His leadership style combined conservative financial management with bold strategic vision. Rather than abandoning the company's gaming heritage entirely, Yamauchi sought to translate Nintendo's understanding of play and entertainment into new technological contexts.

The decision-making process involved several experimental ventures during the 1960s and early 1970s. Nintendo attempted to enter various markets, including instant rice, taxi services, and love hotels. While these diversification attempts were largely unsuccessful, they demonstrated the company's willingness to experiment and search for new opportunities. The key insight came when Yamauchi began to focus on electronic entertainment, recognizing that the fundamental appeal of games could be enhanced through technology.

Executing the Transformation

Nintendo's transformation occurred in several strategic phases. The company first entered the electronic gaming market in the 1970s by securing the rights to distribute the Magnavox Odyssey video game console in Japan. This experience provided valuable insights into the emerging video game market while minimizing initial risk.

The next phase involved developing original electronic games. In 1975, Nintendo partnered with Mitsubishi Electric to create electronic gaming devices. The company hired Gunpei Yokoi, who would become instrumental in Nintendo's future success. Yokoi's creation of the Game & Watch series in 1980 marked Nintendo's first significant success in electronic gaming, demonstrating the company's ability to combine innovative technology with engaging game design.

The transformation accelerated with the development of the Family Computer (Famicom) in Japan in 1983, later released as the Nintendo Entertainment System (NES) in international markets. This console, along with the creation of iconic franchises like Super Mario Bros., solidified Nintendo's position in the video game industry.

Financial and Operational Impact

The financial impact of Nintendo's pivot was extraordinary. By the late 1980s, Nintendo's revenue had grown exponentially compared to its playing card days. The company's market value increased dramatically, and its influence on global entertainment became substantial. The operational transformation required building new capabilities in electronic engineering, software development, and international distribution.

Nintendo maintained its playing card business as a small division, demonstrating respect for its heritage while focusing resources on its new direction. This decision helped maintain organizational stability during the transformation while allowing the company to concentrate on its growing electronic gaming business.

Lessons and Analysis

Nintendo's successful pivot offers several crucial lessons for modern businesses contemplating transformation:

First, the company demonstrated the importance of maintaining core competencies while pivoting to new markets. Nintendo never abandoned its fundamental understanding of what makes games engaging, even as it shifted from cards to electronics.

Second, the transformation highlighted the value of incremental experimentation combined with decisive action. Nintendo tested various markets before committing to electronic gaming, but once the direction was clear, the company pursued it with full commitment.

Third, Nintendo's success in managing the organizational and cultural aspects of transformation was remarkable. The company maintained its focus on quality and innovation while building entirely new technological capabilities.

Perhaps most importantly, Nintendo's pivot shows how companies can remain true to their fundamental purpose while radically changing their business model. The company's transition from playing cards to video games represented not so much an abandonment of its heritage as an evolution of its core mission to provide engaging entertainment.

Looking ahead, Nintendo's transformation continues to offer relevant insights for companies facing technological disruption. The company's ability to identify emerging opportunities while maintaining organizational coherence provides a valuable template for modern business transformation. In an era where technological change continues to accelerate, Nintendo's journey from paper cards to digital entertainment remains a compelling example of successful corporate reinvention.

Chapter 2: Western Union's Evolution: From Telegraph Pioneer to Global Financial Services

Western Union's transformation from a telecommunications giant to a global financial services leader represents one of the most remarkable pivots in business history. The company's journey spans over 170 years, demonstrating extraordinary resilience and adaptability in the face of technological disruption and changing market dynamics.

The Telegraph Empire

Western Union began operations in 1851 as the New York and Mississippi Valley Printing Telegraph Company. Through aggressive expansion and strategic consolidation, the company quickly established itself as America's dominant telegraph service provider. By 1861, Western Union had completed the first transcontinental telegraph line, effectively creating America's first nationwide communications network.

During its telecommunications prime, Western Union's market position was nearly unassailable. The company controlled an extensive network of telegraph lines, offices, and skilled operators across the United States. This infrastructure represented an enormous competitive advantage, making Western Union the primary means of rapid long-distance communication in North America for nearly a century.

The company's original business model was straightforward but highly effective: Western Union charged per message based on distance and word count, operating as both a communication utility and a critical business service. By 1900, the company had become one of the most valuable and influential corporations in America, joining the inaugural Dow Jones Industrial Average.

Catalysts for Transformation

Several factors converged to necessitate Western Union's eventual pivot. The rise of telephone communications in the early 20th century began eroding the telegraph's dominance in personal communications. This erosion accelerated after World War II with the widespread adoption of long-distance telephone services. The final blow to traditional telegraph services came with the advent of digital communications, particularly email and instant messaging in the late 20th century.

However, amid these challenges lay an opportunity that would define Western Union's future. The company's extensive network of offices and its experience in moving information securely across vast distances had given rise to a secondary service: money transfers. This service, initially introduced in

1871 as a complement to messaging, would ultimately become the company's salvation.

Strategic Decision-Making

The transformation of Western Union was not the result of a single decisive moment but rather a series of strategic decisions spanning several decades. In the 1960s and 1970s, company leadership began recognizing that the future of communication would be digital and that traditional telegraph services were becoming obsolete.

The key strategic insight came from analyzing customer behavior patterns. While message volume declined, money transfer services remained robust and even grew in certain markets. Western Union's management recognized that their real competitive advantage lay not in moving messages, but in facilitating secure transactions across a global network.

First Western Financial Corporation's acquisition of Western Union in 1994 marked a crucial turning point. Under new ownership, the company began systematically shifting its focus toward financial services while gradually winding down its traditional telecommunications operations. This transition accelerated under the leadership of Christina Gold, who became CEO in 2006 and championed the company's transformation into a pure-play financial services provider.

Executing the Transformation

Western Union's pivot to financial services occurred through a carefully orchestrated series of steps. The company first expanded its money transfer network globally, leveraging its brand recognition and reputation for reliability. This expansion included establishing partnerships with banks, post offices, and retail locations worldwide.

The company also invested heavily in modernizing its infrastructure, transitioning from physical telegrams to digital systems for processing financial transactions. This technological upgrade was crucial for competing with emerging financial technology companies and traditional banks.

Western Union officially discontinued its telegram service in 2006, marking the symbolic end of its telecommunications era. By this point, the company had successfully repositioned itself as a global leader in cross-border money transfers and payments.

The transformation included significant investments in compliance and regulatory systems, as international financial services require adherence to complex regulatory frameworks. Western Union built sophisticated anti-money laundering systems and fraud prevention capabilities, turning regulatory compliance into a competitive advantage.

Financial and Operational Impact

The financial impact of Western Union's transformation has been substantial. While the company's revenue initially declined as telegraph services were phased out, its financial services business has grown consistently. By 2023, Western Union operated in more than 200 countries and territories, processing billions of dollars in transfers annually.

The operational transformation required building entirely new capabilities. The company transitioned from managing telegraph operators and maintaining physical lines to operating a sophisticated digital financial network. This change demanded new expertise in areas such as financial compliance, digital security, and international banking relationships.

Lessons and Analysis

Western Union's successful pivot offers several valuable lessons for companies facing technological disruption:

First, the company demonstrated the importance of identifying and leveraging core competencies that transcend specific technologies. Western Union's true strength lay not in telegraphy itself but in its ability to move information (and value) securely across distances.

Second, the transformation highlights the value of patient, methodical change. Rather than abruptly abandoning its traditional business, Western Union gradually built its financial services capability while managing the decline of its telegraph business.

Third, Western Union's experience shows how companies can turn regulatory complexity to their advantage. By investing heavily in compliance and security, the company created barriers to entry that helped protect its market position in financial services.

The company's pivot also demonstrates the importance of brand adaptability. Western Union successfully transferred its reputation for reliability and trust from telecommunications to financial services, maintaining brand equity while fundamentally changing its business model.

Looking forward, Western Union continues to face challenges from financial technology startups and digital payment systems. However, its successful transformation from a telecommunications giant to a global financial services provider offers enduring lessons about organizational resilience and strategic reinvention. The company's journey demonstrates that even market leaders in declining industries can successfully pivot if they correctly identify their core strengths and methodically build new capabilities around them.

Chapter 3: Nokia's Journey: From Rubber Boots to Mobile Telecommunications

Few corporate transformations better exemplify the potential for radical reinvention than Nokia's evolution from a Finnish rubber manufacturer to a global telecommunications leader. This remarkable journey, spanning over 150 years, demonstrates how a company can successfully pivot multiple times while maintaining its entrepreneurial spirit and innovative culture.

Industrial Roots and Early Market Position

In 1865, mining engineer Fredrik Idestam established a pulp mill on the banks of the Nokianvirta River in southern Finland, laying the foundation for what would become Nokia Corporation. The company's early years were marked by steady expansion in the paper industry, but its first major transformation came in 1898 with the establishment of Finnish Rubber Works, which later became part of Nokia.

During the early 20th century, Nokia established itself as Finland's premier manufacturer of rubber products, ranging from galoshes and industrial components to tires. The company's market position was particularly strong in the Nordic region, where its rubber boots became a household name. This success was built on quality manufacturing and deep understanding of local market needs.

The company further diversified in 1912 by establishing Finnish Cable Works, producing electrical cables for power transmission and telecommunications. This seemingly modest expansion would later prove crucial in Nokia's transformation. By the 1960s, Nokia operated as a conglomerate encompassing paper, rubber, and cable divisions, with each unit holding significant market share in their respective industries.

Catalysts for Change

Several factors converged in the 1960s and 1970s to necessitate Nokia's strategic transformation. The globalization of manufacturing was intensifying competition in traditional industrial sectors, while the emergence of electronics and digital technology was creating new market opportunities. Finland's economic modernization also played a crucial role, as the country sought to transition from resource-based industries to technology-driven sectors.

A pivotal moment came in the late 1960s when Nokia's cable division began experimenting with radio and telecommunications equipment. The Soviet Union, then Finland's largest trading partner, required sophisticated radio communication systems, providing Nokia with early opportunities in telecommunications technology.

The oil crisis of the 1970s further accelerated the need for change, as it dramatically impacted the economics of Nokia's traditional manufacturing businesses. This external pressure coincided with internal recognition that the future lay in emerging technologies rather than traditional manufacturing.

Strategic Decision-Making

The transformation of Nokia was largely orchestrated by Kari Kairamo, who became CEO in 1977. Kairamo recognized that Nokia's future growth potential lay in electronics and telecommunications rather than its traditional industrial businesses. His vision was to transform Nokia into a technology company focused on mobile communications and digital transmission systems.

This strategic pivot was supported by several key executives, including Simo Vuorilehto and Jorma Ollila, who would later become CEO in 1992. The decision-making process involved careful analysis of global technology trends and recognition that Nokia's expertise in radio communications and digital switching could be leveraged in the emerging mobile telecommunications market.

Executing the Transformation

Nokia's transformation occurred in several phases. The first phase, during the 1980s, involved significant investment in electronics and telecommunications while gradually divesting traditional industrial operations. The company acquired several electronics companies and established research and development facilities focused on mobile communication technology.

The second phase, beginning in the early 1990s under Ollila's leadership, saw Nokia focus exclusively on mobile telecommunications. The company made the bold decision to exit all other businesses, including its historic rubber and paper operations. This focus proved prescient as the global mobile phone market was about to experience explosive growth.

Nokia's timing was remarkable. The company positioned itself at the forefront of the GSM standard's development, which would become the global standard for mobile communications. By investing heavily in research and development and maintaining a focus on user-friendly design, Nokia rapidly established itself as a leader in mobile phone technology.

The transformation required building entirely new capabilities in software development, consumer electronics manufacturing, and global marketing. Nokia successfully recruited technical talent and developed innovative product development processes that allowed it to introduce new phone models rapidly.

Financial and Operational Impact

The financial impact of Nokia's transformation was extraordinary. By the late 1990s, Nokia had become Europe's largest company by market capitalization and Finland's largest private employer. The company's revenue grew from approximately $2 billion in 1990 to over $30 billion by 2000, with mobile phones accounting for the majority of sales.

The operational transformation was equally dramatic. Nokia evolved from a traditional manufacturer with primarily Nordic operations to a global technology company with research centers, manufacturing facilities, and sales operations worldwide. The company developed sophisticated supply chain management systems and built strong relationships with telecommunications operators globally.

Lessons and Analysis

Nokia's transformation offers several crucial lessons for companies contemplating fundamental change:

First, the company demonstrated the importance of timing strategic pivots to coincide with emerging technological waves. Nokia's entry into mobile telecommunications aligned perfectly with the global adoption of cellular technology.

Second, Nokia's experience highlights the value of focus and the courage to exit traditional businesses. The decision to divest profitable but non-core operations allowed the company to concentrate resources on its emerging telecommunications business.

Third, the transformation underscores the importance of building new capabilities while maintaining organizational agility. Nokia successfully developed expertise in new technologies while fostering a culture of innovation and quick decision-making.

The company's journey also demonstrates the potential for multiple successful transformations within a single organization. Nokia's evolution from paper to rubber to electronics shows how core competencies in manufacturing excellence and technological innovation can be applied across different industries.

Perhaps most importantly, Nokia's case illustrates how companies can successfully pivot by identifying and investing in emerging technologies that align with their capabilities. The company's expertise in radio communications and digital switching, developed in its cable division, provided a foundation for its success in mobile telecommunications.

While Nokia would later face challenges in the smartphone era, its transformation from a rubber boot manufacturer to a global telecommunications leader remains one of the most remarkable examples of successful corporate reinvention in business history. The company's journey offers enduring lessons about the importance of strategic foresight, focused execution, and organizational adaptation in driving successful business transformation.

Chapter 4: IBM's Strategic Shift: From Hardware Giant to Services Leader

International Business Machines Corporation's transformation from a dominant hardware manufacturer to a global services and consulting leader stands as one of the most significant strategic pivots in corporate history. This metamorphosis not only saved the company from potential obsolescence but established a new paradigm for technology companies facing disruption.

The Hardware Empire

For most of the 20th century, IBM dominated the global computing hardware market. The company's business model centered on the development, manufacture, and sale of mainframe computers, with complementary revenue streams from hardware maintenance and support. IBM's market position was so commanding that it faced antitrust scrutiny, with the U.S. Department of Justice referring to it as a "national problem" in the 1970s.

By the 1980s, IBM controlled approximately 70% of the mainframe computer market. The company's success was built on vertical integration, proprietary technology, and a reputation for unparalleled reliability, encapsulated in the saying "Nobody ever got fired for buying IBM." This business model generated extraordinary profits, with hardware sales and associated maintenance contracts providing predictable, high-margin revenue streams.

Catalysts for Transformation

The early 1990s brought unprecedented challenges to IBM's traditional business model. The rise of personal computers and distributed computing began eroding the mainframe market. New competitors like Microsoft and Intel were capturing value in the PC era through software and processors, while hardware was becoming increasingly commoditized.

IBM's financial results reflected these challenges dramatically. The company's revenue declined precipitously between 1991 and 1993, culminating in a staggering $8.1 billion loss in 1993—then the largest in American corporate history. Market analysts began questioning IBM's survival, and the company's stock price plummeted.

The technological shift toward client-server computing and the internet was fundamentally changing how businesses utilized technology. Companies needed help integrating various technologies and systems rather than simply purchasing hardware. This market evolution created an opportunity for a new type of technology services provider.

Strategic Decision-Making

In 1993, IBM's board made the crucial decision to hire Louis V. Gerstner Jr. as CEO—the first outsider to lead the company in its history. Gerstner's appointment was controversial; as the former head of RJR Nabisco and American Express, he lacked traditional technology industry experience. However, his background as a customer of technology would prove invaluable in reshaping IBM's strategy.

Gerstner's initial analysis revealed that IBM's customers weren't merely seeking hardware solutions; they needed help solving complex business problems through technology. This insight led to the strategic decision to build a global technology services business, leveraging IBM's deep technical expertise and trusted relationship with enterprise customers.

The decision-making process involved extensive customer consultation and internal debate. Many IBM veterans advocated breaking up the company into smaller, more focused units. Gerstner, however, recognized that IBM's greatest strength lay in its ability to provide integrated solutions to complex problems—a capability that would be lost if the company were dismantled.

Executing the Transformation

The transformation of IBM required fundamental changes across multiple dimensions. First, the company reorganized its operations around customer needs rather than product lines. This involved creating integrated teams that could draw upon IBM's full range of capabilities to solve customer problems.

IBM made several strategic acquisitions to build its consulting capabilities, including the purchase of PricewaterhouseCoopers Consulting in 2002 for $3.5 billion. This acquisition added crucial business consulting expertise to complement IBM's technical capabilities.

The company also invested heavily in developing its Global Services division, which grew from a relatively small unit to become IBM's largest business segment.

This growth required significant changes in hiring practices, compensation systems, and corporate culture to support a services-led business model.

The transformation extended to IBM's sales approach. The company moved from transaction-based hardware sales to building long-term service relationships with clients. This shift required retraining thousands of sales professionals and developing new compensation models that rewarded long-term client relationships rather than individual transactions.

Financial and Operational Impact

The financial impact of IBM's transformation was remarkable. By 2001, services accounted for more than 40% of IBM's revenue and generated higher profit margins than hardware. The company's market value increased substantially, and IBM regained its position as a technology industry leader, albeit in a very different form.

Operationally, the transformation required building entirely new capabilities in consulting, system integration, and managed services. IBM evolved from a manufacturing-focused organization to one primarily focused on services delivery and client relationship management. This shift involved significant changes in workforce composition, with the company hiring thousands of consultants and services professionals while reducing its manufacturing workforce.

Lessons and Analysis

IBM's successful transformation offers several crucial lessons for companies facing technological disruption:

First, the company demonstrated the importance of listening to customers and understanding their fundamental needs rather than focusing solely on protecting existing product lines. Gerstner's outsider perspective helped IBM recognize that customers valued solutions more than specific technologies.

Second, IBM's experience highlights the value of maintaining organizational coherence during transformation. Rather than breaking up the company, IBM leveraged its scale and integrated capabilities to build a stronger competitive position in services.

Third, the transformation underscores the importance of cultural change in enabling strategic shifts. IBM successfully evolved from a culture focused on technical superiority to one centered on client service and solution delivery.

The company's pivot also demonstrates how traditional strengths can be repurposed for new markets. IBM's deep technical expertise and strong client relationships, originally built through hardware sales, became valuable assets in its services business.

Looking forward, IBM's transformation continues to offer relevant insights for companies facing technological disruption. The company's ability to reinvent itself while maintaining its core values of innovation and customer service provides a valuable template for corporate renewal. As technology continues to evolve, IBM's journey from hardware manufacturer to services leader remains a compelling example of successful strategic transformation.

Chapter 5: Marvel Entertainment: From Bankruptcy to Entertainment Powerhouse

Marvel Entertainment's transformation from a bankrupt comic book publisher to a global entertainment empire represents one of the most remarkable corporate turnarounds in recent history. The company's journey demonstrates how intellectual property, when properly leveraged, can drive extraordinary business value and enable dramatic strategic pivots.

Origins and Initial Market Position

Marvel's original business model was straightforward: publish comic books and license characters for basic merchandise. Founded in 1939 as Timely Publications, the company that would become Marvel Comics had created an extraordinary catalog of characters, including Spider-Man, the X-Men, and the Fantastic Four. By the 1980s, Marvel dominated the comic book market alongside DC Comics, with a devoted following but limited revenue streams.

The company relied primarily on two sources of income: comic book sales and basic licensing deals for toys and merchandise. While this model had sustained the business for decades, it left significant value untapped in Marvel's vast intellectual property portfolio. The comic book industry itself was relatively small, with limited growth potential in traditional publishing formats.

Catalysts for Change

Marvel's path to transformation began with a crisis. In 1996, following years of mismanagement, declining comic book sales, and the collapse of the speculative comic book market, Marvel filed for Chapter 11 bankruptcy protection. The company's stock, which had traded as high as $35 per share in 1993, plummeted to pennies. The bankruptcy filing marked the nadir of Marvel's fortunes but also created the conditions for its reinvention.

A second crucial catalyst emerged from observing the success of other companies in monetizing comic book properties. The commercial success of films like Blade (1998) and X-Men (2000) demonstrated the potential value of Marvel's character library in other media formats. These early successes, achieved through traditional licensing arrangements, suggested that Marvel was significantly undervaluing its intellectual property.

Strategic Decision-Making

The key architects of Marvel's transformation emerged during and after the bankruptcy reorganization. Isaac Perlmutter and Avi Arad played crucial roles in recognizing the untapped potential of Marvel's character library. However, it was the appointment of David Maisel as Chairman of Marvel Studios and the strategic vision of CEO Peter Cuneo that truly catalyzed the company's transformation.

The pivotal strategic decision was to move from a pure licensing model to becoming an independent film producer. This decision was controversial and risky, requiring significant capital investment and the development of entirely new capabilities. The leadership team recognized that while licensing deals provided steady income, they prevented Marvel from capturing the full value of its intellectual property.

In 2005, Marvel made the bold decision to self-finance its films, arranging a $525 million financing facility with Merrill Lynch. This decision gave Marvel complete creative control over its properties and the potential to capture substantially more value from successful films.

Executing the Transformation

The execution of Marvel's transformation occurred in several phases. First, the company needed to stabilize its core publishing business while maintaining valuable licensing relationships. This provided the financial foundation for more ambitious initiatives.

The second phase involved developing internal capabilities in film production and creative development. Marvel established Marvel Studios, hiring experienced film industry executives and creating a creative committee to ensure consistency across various projects. The company also developed a sophisticated approach to universe-building, planning interconnected films that would become the Marvel Cinematic Universe (MCU).

The execution strategy was methodical. Marvel began with Iron Man, a character that was well-known to comic fans but not considered one of their premier properties. This reduced the risk while allowing the company to establish its film-making capabilities. The success of Iron Man in 2008 validated Marvel's approach and set the stage for more ambitious projects.

The company also implemented a rigorous approach to talent management, signing actors to multi-picture deals and maintaining creative consistency across films. This strategy helped build a coherent cinematic universe that would become increasingly valuable over time.

Financial and Operational Impact

The financial impact of Marvel's transformation has been extraordinary. The company's value increased from bankruptcy in 1996 to a $4 billion acquisition by Disney in 2009. The MCU has generated over $25 billion in box office revenue, becoming the most successful film franchise in history.

Operationally, Marvel evolved from a publishing company with a licensing division to a sophisticated entertainment company capable of producing multiple blockbuster films per year. The company developed new capabilities in film production, marketing, and franchise management while maintaining its traditional publishing and licensing businesses.

Lessons and Analysis

Marvel's transformation offers several crucial lessons for companies considering strategic pivots:

First, the company demonstrated the importance of recognizing and properly valuing core assets. Marvel's true value lay not in its publishing business but in its intellectual property and storytelling capabilities.

Second, the transformation highlights the value of vertical integration in capturing intellectual property value. By moving from licensing to production, Marvel dramatically increased its share of the value created by its properties.

Third, Marvel's experience shows how companies can use crisis as a catalyst for reinvention. The bankruptcy, while painful, created conditions that enabled radical strategic change.

The company's success also demonstrates the importance of patient, methodical execution in transformation. Marvel built its cinematic universe carefully, focusing on quality and consistency rather than rushing to exploit its most valuable properties.

Looking forward, Marvel's transformation continues to influence how companies think about intellectual property and entertainment franchises. The company's success in building an interconnected cinematic universe has created a new model for entertainment companies and demonstrated how traditional media properties can be reimagined for modern audiences.

The Marvel case also illustrates how companies can successfully pivot by identifying their core value proposition—in this case, storytelling and character development—and finding new ways to monetize it. While few companies possess a character library as valuable as Marvel's, the principles of identifying and leveraging core intellectual property assets are broadly applicable across industries.

Chapter 6: Netflix: The Strategic Evolution from DVD Rentals to Streaming Giant

The transformation of Netflix from a DVD-by-mail rental service to the world's leading streaming platform represents one of the most prescient and well-executed pivots in business history. This evolution demonstrates how companies can successfully navigate technological disruption by anticipating market changes and making bold strategic moves, even when such decisions might temporarily disadvantage their core business.

Origins and Initial Market Position

When Netflix launched in 1997, it entered the video rental market with an innovative yet straightforward business model: DVD rentals by mail with no late fees. The company's initial value proposition addressed significant consumer pain points in the traditional video rental market, particularly the inconvenience of store visits and the frustration of late fees.

By 2005, Netflix had built a substantial DVD subscription business with over 4.2 million members. The company's competitive advantages included sophisticated logistics operations, proprietary recommendation algorithms, and a vast selection of titles. Netflix's efficient distribution network of regional warehouses enabled next-day delivery to most customers, while its recommendation system helped subscribers discover content aligned with their interests.

This business model proved highly successful in competing against traditional brick-and-mortar rental chains, particularly Blockbuster. Netflix's subscription approach generated predictable recurring revenue, while its no-late-fees policy and convenient home delivery resonated strongly with consumers. The company had effectively digitized the rental process while still operating within the constraints of physical media distribution.

Catalysts for Transformation

Several factors influenced Netflix's decision to pivot toward streaming. First, the company's leadership recognized that improvements in internet infrastructure and video compression technology would eventually make streaming video commercially viable. Reed Hastings, Netflix's co-founder and CEO, had originally conceived of streaming as the company's ultimate destination, viewing the DVD-by-mail service as an intermediate step.

The rise of YouTube in 2005 demonstrated consumer appetite for streaming video content, albeit in short-form format. Additionally, the increasing adoption of broadband internet and the proliferation of internet-connected devices suggested that the technological foundation for streaming was approaching maturity.

Perhaps most importantly, Netflix's leadership recognized that physical DVD distribution, while profitable, would eventually face technological obsolescence. The threat of digital disruption was not immediate—DVD rentals remained popular and profitable—but the writing was on the wall for physical media.

Strategic Decision-Making

The decision to pursue streaming was championed by Reed Hastings and his executive team, particularly Ted Sarandos, who would later become co-CEO. The strategic planning process involved careful analysis of technological trends, consumer behavior, and competitive dynamics.

A crucial insight was that streaming would eventually offer significant advantages over physical distribution: instant access to content, lower distribution costs, and the ability to gather detailed viewing data to inform content recommendations and acquisitions. However, the transition would require massive investments in technology infrastructure and content licensing.

The decision-making process was marked by intense debate about timing and execution. Moving too quickly risked alienating DVD subscribers and incurring unsustainable content costs, while moving too slowly risked losing first-mover advantage in streaming. The company ultimately decided to pursue an aggressive transition while maintaining its DVD service as a separate business unit.

Executing the Transformation

Netflix launched its streaming service in 2007, initially offering it as a free add-on to DVD subscriptions. This approach allowed the company to build streaming adoption while maintaining its profitable DVD business. The early streaming catalog was limited, but it provided valuable insights into consumer behavior and technical requirements.

The transformation accelerated in 2011 when Netflix made the controversial decision to separate its DVD and streaming services, effectively raising prices for customers who wanted both services. While this decision initially sparked significant customer backlash, it reflected the company's commitment to streaming as its future.

A crucial element of the transformation was Netflix's move into original content production. Recognizing that relying solely on licensed content would leave the company vulnerable to content owners' streaming ambitions, Netflix began producing original series with "House of Cards" in 2013. This vertical integration into content production represented a second major pivot within the broader streaming transformation.

The execution also involved building substantial new capabilities in technology and content production. Netflix invested heavily in its streaming infrastructure, developing sophisticated content delivery networks and adaptive streaming technologies. The company also built new capabilities in content development, production, and global distribution.

Financial and Operational Impact

The financial impact of Netflix's transformation has been extraordinary. The company's revenue grew from approximately $1.2 billion in 2007 to over $25 billion by 2020. Market capitalization increased dramatically as investors recognized the global scalability of the streaming model.

Operationally, Netflix evolved from a logistics-focused DVD distribution company to a technology and entertainment company. This required significant changes in workforce composition, with the company adding substantial engineering and creative talent while gradually reducing its DVD operations.

The transformation also enabled global expansion. While DVD rental was inherently limited to the United States, streaming allowed Netflix to expand rapidly into international markets, eventually reaching over 190 countries.

Lessons and Analysis

Netflix's successful transformation offers several crucial lessons for companies facing technological disruption:

The experience demonstrates the importance of proactive transformation, even when current operations remain profitable. Netflix began its streaming pivot while its DVD business was still growing, recognizing that waiting for decline would leave too little time for successful transformation.

The company's approach to managing the transition period was instructive. By initially offering streaming as a complement to DVD service, Netflix was able to build streaming adoption while maintaining DVD revenue. This "bridge" strategy provided financial stability during the transformation period.

Netflix's experience also highlights the importance of continuous innovation. The company did not stop with the transition to streaming but continued to evolve by moving into original content production and international markets. This willingness to keep transforming has been crucial to maintaining competitive advantage.

The transformation also demonstrates the value of maintaining strategic focus. Despite opportunities to diversify into adjacent businesses, Netflix remained focused on its core mission of entertainment delivery, albeit through evolving technologies.

Looking forward, Netflix's journey offers enduring lessons about the importance of anticipating technological change and making bold strategic moves to address it. The company's willingness to disrupt its own successful business model, rather than waiting for competitors to do so, provides a template for proactive strategic transformation in the digital age.

Chapter 7: Fujifilm's Digital Response: Why It Succeeded Where Kodak Failed

In the annals of corporate transformation, few stories offer more striking contrasts than the divergent paths taken by Fujifilm and Kodak in response to the digital photography revolution. While both companies faced identical technological disruption, Fujifilm's successful pivot and Kodak's eventual bankruptcy provide a compelling case study in adaptive corporate strategy and organizational resilience.

Origins and Market Position

Fujifilm, established in 1934, built its business on photographic film, competing globally with Kodak in both consumer and professional markets. While Kodak dominated the American market with approximately 70% market share, Fujifilm maintained a strong position in Asia and gradually expanded its presence in Western markets through competitive pricing and innovation in film quality.

By the 1980s, Fujifilm had established itself as a formidable competitor in the global photographic market, with a comprehensive portfolio including film, cameras, processing equipment, and photographic paper. The company's market position was built on technical excellence, particularly in color reproduction and film durability. However, like Kodak, Fujifilm relied heavily on the traditional photography business, with photographic products accounting for approximately 60% of its revenue.

Catalysts for Transformation

The advent of digital photography presented an existential threat to the traditional photography industry. Early warning signs appeared in the 1980s with the introduction of early digital cameras, but the true disruption accelerated in the late 1990s as digital camera technology improved and prices declined. Fujifilm's leadership recognized that digital technology would eventually obsolete traditional photographic film, a conclusion that demanded decisive action.

A crucial catalyst came from careful analysis of market data. Between 2000 and 2010, global demand for photographic film dropped by approximately 90%. This precipitous decline was far more rapid than many industry observers had predicted, creating urgency for transformation. Unlike Kodak, which viewed this decline primarily as a threat, Fujifilm's leadership saw it as an opportunity for fundamental reinvention.

Strategic Decision-Making

Under the leadership of CEO Shigetaka Komori, who assumed the position in 2000, Fujifilm developed a comprehensive transformation strategy. Komori's approach was based on two key insights: first, that the decline of traditional photography was irreversible, and second, that Fujifilm's core technologies could be applied to other industries.

The strategic planning process involved a systematic analysis of Fujifilm's technological capabilities. The company identified that its expertise in areas such as collagen, nanoparticles, and thin-film coating had applications far beyond photography. This analysis led to the identification of several promising markets, including healthcare, cosmetics, and high-performance materials.

A crucial decision was to maintain significant R&D investment despite declining revenues from the traditional business. This contrasted sharply with Kodak's approach of reducing R&D spending to protect short-term profitability. Fujifilm's leadership recognized that new growth would require both technological innovation and acquisitions.

Executing the Transformation

Fujifilm's transformation was executed through a series of carefully planned initiatives. The company first moved to protect cash flow from its existing photography business through aggressive cost reduction and efficiency improvements. This generated resources to fund the transformation while maintaining profitability.

The company then pursued a two-pronged growth strategy. First, it leveraged its expertise in digital imaging to build positions in adjacent markets such as medical imaging, printing, and document solutions. Second, it identified new applications for its core technologies in emerging markets such as pharmaceuticals and electronic materials.

Fujifilm made several strategic acquisitions to accelerate its transformation. The 2006 acquisition of Toyama Chemical strengthened its position in pharmaceuticals, while the purchase of various healthcare and cosmetics companies expanded its presence in these growing markets. The company also invested heavily in internal R&D to develop new applications for its proprietary technologies.

A crucial element of the execution was maintaining organizational cohesion during the transformation. Fujifilm worked to retain key technical talent while retraining employees for new roles. The company's strong corporate culture, centered on innovation and adaptation, proved valuable in managing this transition.

Financial and Operational Impact

The financial results of Fujifilm's transformation have been remarkable. While the company's traditional photography business declined dramatically, new businesses in healthcare, highly functional materials, and document solutions grew to represent over 80% of revenue by 2020. The company's market value increased substantially, and profitability remained stable during the transformation.

Operationally, Fujifilm evolved from a photography company to a diversified technology company with leading positions in multiple high-growth markets. The company successfully transferred core capabilities in chemistry, materials science, and precision manufacturing to new applications while developing new capabilities in pharmaceuticals and healthcare.

Lessons and Analysis

Fujifilm's successful transformation offers several crucial lessons for companies facing technological disruption:

First, the company demonstrated the importance of proactive transformation. Rather than waiting for the photography market to collapse, Fujifilm began its pivot while still generating substantial profits from traditional products. This provided resources and time for successful transformation.

Second, Fujifilm's experience highlights the value of deep technological capabilities. The company's success in new markets was built on its ability to repurpose core technologies for new applications. This suggests that companies facing disruption should carefully inventory their technological assets for potential new applications.

Third, the transformation underscores the importance of maintaining R&D investment during periods of change. Fujifilm's continued commitment to innovation, even as its traditional market declined, enabled its successful entry into new markets.

The contrast with Kodak is instructive. While Kodak focused primarily on preserving its existing business model and transitioning to digital photography, Fujifilm pursued a broader transformation that leveraged its core technologies in entirely new markets. This more fundamental reinvention proved more successful than Kodak's narrower digital transition strategy.

Looking forward, Fujifilm's transformation offers enduring lessons about the importance of technological adaptation and business model innovation. The company's ability to identify new applications for existing capabilities while developing new ones provides a valuable template for corporate renewal in the face of technological disruption.

Chapter 8: Amazon: From Online Bookstore to Everything Store and Cloud Computing Leader

Amazon's transformation from an online bookstore to a global technology and retail powerhouse represents one of the most ambitious and successful corporate pivots in business history. The company's journey demonstrates how continuous innovation and strategic expansion can transform a focused online retailer into a diversified technology leader that reshapes multiple industries.

Origins and Initial Market Position

When Amazon launched in 1994, Jeff Bezos positioned the company as "Earth's Biggest Bookstore," choosing books as the initial product category due to their uniform nature, established distribution systems, and vast selection. The company's original business model centered on providing a superior online book-buying experience, offering customers unprecedented selection and convenience.

Amazon's initial value proposition was straightforward but compelling: provide access to millions of books through an easy-to-use website, with competitive prices and direct-to-home delivery. The company quickly established itself as the leading online bookseller, leveraging the internet's ability to offer virtually unlimited inventory without the physical constraints of traditional bookstores.

By 1997, Amazon had achieved significant scale in online book sales, but this represented only a small fraction of the overall retail market. The company's early success was built on superior customer experience, efficient operations, and rapid growth in the nascent e-commerce sector. However, the limitations of remaining solely a book retailer were already apparent to leadership.

Catalysts for Transformation

Several factors drove Amazon's strategic evolution. First, the company recognized that its core competencies in e-commerce—inventory management, fulfillment, and customer service—could be applied to other retail categories. The success in books demonstrated the viability of online retail for products beyond media.

A second crucial catalyst emerged from Amazon's internal technology needs. The company had developed sophisticated systems to manage its rapidly growing e-commerce operations. This infrastructure development led to the recognition that other businesses might value similar capabilities, eventually inspiring the creation of Amazon Web Services (AWS).

Perhaps most importantly, Bezos and his team realized that remaining focused solely on books would limit Amazon's growth potential and increase vulnerability to competition. The emergence of other e-commerce players demonstrated that the barriers to entry in online retail were relatively low, creating pressure for diversification.

Strategic Decision-Making

The transformation of Amazon was guided by Jeff Bezos's leadership and his philosophy of customer obsession and long-term thinking. Key strategic decisions were driven by several core principles: prioritize customer value over short-term profits, continuously innovate and experiment, and build scalable platforms rather than individual products.

The decision to expand beyond books was made relatively early, but the company approached this expansion methodically. Each new category was selected based on its potential for online sales and Amazon's ability to add unique value. The progression from books to music and video, and then to electronics and other categories, followed a deliberate pattern of testing and learning.

The creation of AWS represented an even more dramatic strategic pivot. The decision to offer Amazon's internal technology infrastructure as a service to other companies was both innovative and risky. This move required significant investment and represented a departure from the company's retail focus, but leadership recognized the enormous potential of cloud computing.

Executing the Transformation

Amazon's transformation occurred through a series of carefully planned expansions and innovations. The company first established dominance in media products (books, music, and video) before gradually expanding into other retail categories. This expansion required building new capabilities in product sourcing, inventory management, and category-specific customer service.

The launch of Amazon Marketplace in 2000 represented another crucial transformation, allowing third-party sellers to use Amazon's platform. This move dramatically expanded product selection while sharing inventory risk with partners. The development of Fulfillment by Amazon (FBA) further enhanced this strategy by providing logistics services to marketplace sellers.

The launch of AWS in 2006 marked Amazon's most significant pivot. The company leveraged its expertise in building scalable technology infrastructure to create a new business model in cloud computing. AWS required building new capabilities in enterprise sales and support while maintaining the rapid innovation pace that characterized Amazon's retail operations.

Amazon's transformation also included significant investments in logistics and fulfillment. The company built a vast network of warehouses and distribution centers, developed proprietary robotics technology, and eventually created its own delivery network.

These investments enabled Amazon to control the entire customer experience while reducing dependence on third-party carriers.

Financial and Operational Impact

The financial impact of Amazon's transformation has been extraordinary. The company grew from $147 million in revenue in 1997 to over $386 billion in 2020. More significantly, AWS became the company's most profitable division, generating operating margins far higher than retail operations.

Operationally, Amazon evolved from a focused online retailer to a complex organization managing multiple business models. The company developed sophisticated capabilities in technology, logistics, digital media, and enterprise services. This diversification reduced business risk while creating multiple growth engines.

Lessons and Analysis

Amazon's transformation offers several crucial lessons for companies contemplating strategic evolution:

The company demonstrated the importance of maintaining a consistent corporate culture and strategic principles while pursuing new opportunities. Amazon's focus on customer value and long-term thinking provided a framework for evaluating and executing new initiatives.

The transformation highlights the value of building platforms rather than individual products. Amazon's most successful pivots—Marketplace and AWS—

involved creating platforms that other businesses could build upon, multiplying their impact and value.

Amazon's experience also shows how companies can leverage internal capabilities to create new business opportunities. AWS emerged from Amazon's need to solve its own technology challenges, demonstrating how internal solutions can become valuable external offerings.

The company's approach to transformation emphasizes the importance of patient capital and willingness to endure short-term losses for long-term value creation. Amazon consistently prioritized growth and customer value over immediate profitability, a strategy that required both investor support and leadership conviction.

Looking forward, Amazon's journey offers enduring lessons about the importance of continuous innovation and strategic experimentation. The company's ability to enter and reshape multiple industries while maintaining operational excellence provides a template for ambitious corporate transformation in the digital age.

Chapter 9: Microsoft's Cloud Revolution: Redefining Success in the Post-PC Era

Microsoft's transformation from a desktop software company to a cloud computing leader represents one of the most successful strategic pivots in technology history. The company's journey demonstrates how a dominant market leader can reinvent itself in response to technological disruption while maintaining its core mission of empowering productivity through technology.

Origins and Market Position

By the early 2000s, Microsoft had established an extraordinarily powerful market position built on two primary pillars: the Windows operating system and the Office productivity suite. This duopoly generated consistent high-margin revenue through a perpetual licensing model, with Microsoft controlling approximately 95% of the operating system market for personal computers and a similar share in office productivity software.

The company's business model was fundamentally based on selling software licenses for desktop computers, with regular upgrades driving recurring revenue. This model had proven enormously profitable, making Microsoft one of the world's most valuable companies. The company's market position was further strengthened by strong network effects and high switching costs for both individual and enterprise customers.

However, this very success created organizational inertia and a resistance to change that would eventually threaten Microsoft's market position. The company's culture and infrastructure were optimized for delivering packaged software products through traditional channels, making it initially slow to respond to cloud-based threats.

Catalysts for Transformation

Several factors converged to necessitate Microsoft's strategic pivot toward cloud computing. The rise of mobile computing and smartphones challenged the dominance of personal computers as the primary computing platform. Apple's iPhone and Google's Android operating system created new platforms where Microsoft had limited presence.

The emergence of cloud-based productivity tools, particularly Google Apps (now Google Workspace), presented a direct threat to Microsoft's Office franchise. These tools offered collaboration capabilities that were difficult to replicate with traditional desktop software and appealed particularly to younger users and new businesses.

Perhaps most significantly, Amazon's success with AWS demonstrated the enormous potential of cloud infrastructure services. Enterprise customers were increasingly moving their computing workloads to the cloud, threatening Microsoft's traditional enterprise software business.

Strategic Decision-Making

The appointment of Satya Nadella as CEO in 2014 marked a crucial turning point in Microsoft's transformation. Nadella, who had previously led Microsoft's cloud and enterprise group, brought deep understanding of cloud technology and a fresh perspective on Microsoft's strategic position.

Nadella and his leadership team made several key strategic decisions that would shape Microsoft's transformation. First, they committed to making

Microsoft's products available across all platforms, moving beyond the traditional Windows-first approach. Second, they shifted from a perpetual licensing model to a subscription-based model for key products. Third, they prioritized cloud infrastructure investment, positioning Azure as a central element of Microsoft's future.

The decision-making process was guided by Nadella's vision of Microsoft as a platform and productivity company for the mobile-first, cloud-first world. This represented a significant departure from the company's traditional focus on Windows and desktop software while maintaining its core mission of empowering productivity.

Executing the Transformation

The execution of Microsoft's cloud transformation occurred across multiple dimensions. The company first moved its Office productivity suite to the cloud with Office 365, offering subscription-based access and enhanced collaboration features. This transition required significant changes to development processes, sales approaches, and customer support models.

The development of Azure represented an even more ambitious transformation. Microsoft leveraged its enterprise relationships and understanding of business computing needs to build a comprehensive cloud platform. The company made substantial investments in data centers and networking infrastructure while developing new capabilities in areas like artificial intelligence and edge computing.

Microsoft also pursued strategic acquisitions to accelerate its transformation. The purchase of LinkedIn provided valuable professional network data and enterprise relationships. The acquisition of GitHub strengthened Microsoft's position with developers and demonstrated its commitment to open-source software, marking a dramatic shift from its historical approach.

The transformation extended to Microsoft's culture and operating model. Nadella promoted a growth mindset culture, encouraging experimentation and learning from failure. The company restructured its organization around cloud services and adopted agile development practices across its product portfolio.

Financial and Operational Impact

The financial results of Microsoft's transformation have been remarkable. The company's market value increased dramatically under Nadella's leadership, driven by strong growth in cloud services. Azure revenue grew at double-digit rates for multiple consecutive quarters, while Office 365 successfully transitioned the productivity business to a subscription model.

Operationally, Microsoft evolved from a software product company to a cloud services provider. This required developing new capabilities in areas like data center operations, network management, and service reliability. The company also built new sales and support capabilities focused on cloud services and subscription relationships.

Lessons and Analysis

Microsoft's successful transformation offers several crucial lessons for established companies facing technological disruption:

The experience demonstrates the importance of leadership in driving organizational change. Nadella's ability to articulate a compelling vision while respecting Microsoft's heritage helped overcome internal resistance to change.

The transformation highlights the value of maintaining customer relationships during business model transitions. Microsoft successfully leveraged its enterprise relationships to build its cloud business while carefully managing the transition from perpetual licenses to subscriptions.

Microsoft's approach also shows how companies can use their existing strengths to advantage in new markets. The company's understanding of enterprise computing needs and developer tools provided valuable insights for building Azure and cloud services.

Looking forward, Microsoft's journey offers enduring lessons about the importance of strategic adaptation in the face of technological change. The company's ability to transform its business model while maintaining its core mission provides a template for established companies seeking to navigate digital transformation.

The success of Microsoft's cloud pivot also demonstrates how traditional competitive advantages can be reimagined for new technological paradigms. While the nature of Microsoft's advantages changed from desktop software to cloud services, the company's fundamental strengths in enterprise relationships and developer tools remained relevant and valuable.

Chapter 10: Adobe: The Brilliant Shift from Boxed Software to Cloud Subscriptions

Adobe's transformation from a traditional software vendor to a cloud-based subscription service provider stands as one of the most successful business model pivots in the software industry. This transformation not only secured Adobe's market position but also created a new standard for software distribution and pricing that would influence the entire industry.

Origins and Market Position

Prior to its transformation, Adobe dominated the creative software market with industry-standard products like Photoshop, Illustrator, and InDesign. The company's business model was built on selling perpetual licenses for its Creative Suite, with major version updates released approximately every 18 months. This model generated substantial revenue through initial purchases and upgrade cycles, with Adobe controlling approximately 90% of the professional creative software market.

Adobe's market position was fortified by high switching costs, as creative professionals invested significant time in learning the company's complex software tools. Additionally, Adobe's PDF format and Acrobat software had become the global standard for document sharing, providing another stable revenue stream. The company's products were sold primarily through retail channels and enterprise licensing agreements, with prices ranging from hundreds to thousands of dollars per license.

However, this business model had inherent limitations. The high upfront costs created barriers to adoption, particularly for smaller businesses and individual creators. The lengthy upgrade cycle meant that revenue was lumpy and somewhat unpredictable, while also slowing the pace of innovation as major features were held back for version releases.

Catalysts for Transformation

Several factors drove Adobe's decision to transform its business model. The rise of cloud computing and software-as-a-service (SaaS) was changing customer expectations about software delivery and pricing. Companies like Salesforce had demonstrated the viability of the subscription model for enterprise software, while consumer services like Netflix had familiarized users with subscription pricing.

Software piracy presented another significant challenge, particularly in emerging markets where high license costs made legal purchases prohibitive for many users. The company estimated that for every paid copy of Creative Suite, there were multiple unauthorized copies in use.

Perhaps most importantly, Adobe's leadership recognized that the traditional software release cycle was becoming incompatible with the rapid pace of technological change. The explosion of mobile devices and new content formats required more frequent updates and better integration across creative tools.

Strategic Decision-Making

The pivot to a subscription model was championed by Shantanu Narayen, who became CEO in 2007. Narayen and his team recognized that moving to the cloud would not only address immediate challenges but also create new opportunities for product innovation and market expansion.

The decision-making process involved careful analysis of potential risks and benefits. The transition would require significant investment in cloud infrastructure and would likely result in short-term revenue decline as the company shifted from large upfront payments to smaller monthly subscriptions. There were also concerns about customer resistance to the new model, particularly among enterprise customers with established purchasing patterns.

However, Adobe's leadership concluded that the long-term benefits outweighed the risks. A subscription model would provide more predictable revenue, reduce piracy, lower barriers to adoption, and enable faster innovation through continuous delivery of new features.

Executing the Transformation

Adobe began its transformation in 2012 with the launch of Creative Cloud, offering subscription access to its creative software suite. The execution strategy involved several key elements:

Adobe maintained its existing Creative Suite products during the initial transition period while gradually adding exclusive features to Creative Cloud. This approach provided customers with time to adjust while creating incentives for early adoption of the new model.

The company invested heavily in cloud infrastructure and new development capabilities to support continuous software delivery. This required significant changes to development processes, moving from large periodic releases to smaller, more frequent updates.

Adobe also expanded its product portfolio, adding new tools and services that would have been difficult to deliver under the traditional model. Mobile apps and cross-device synchronization became key features of the Creative Cloud offering.

The transformation extended to Adobe's sales and marketing operations. The company built new capabilities in subscription sales and customer success management while developing analytics to monitor customer usage and reduce churn.

Financial and Operational Impact

The financial impact of Adobe's transformation exceeded expectations. After an initial period of revenue decline as the company shifted to subscriptions, Adobe's recurring revenue and overall profitability increased substantially. The company's market value grew significantly, reflecting investor confidence in the subscription model.

Operationally, Adobe evolved from a product-centered organization to a service-oriented one. This required new capabilities in areas like cloud operations, customer success, and usage analytics.

The company also achieved better visibility into customer behavior and needs, enabling more targeted product development.

Lessons and Analysis

Adobe's successful transformation offers several crucial lessons for companies considering business model changes:

The experience demonstrates the importance of decisive leadership in driving fundamental business model changes. Despite risks and potential customer resistance, Adobe's management maintained commitment to the transformation while carefully managing the transition period.

The transformation highlights the value of customer relationships during business model transitions. Adobe successfully communicated the benefits of the new model while providing tools and support to help customers adapt.

Adobe's approach also shows how companies can use business model innovation to address multiple strategic challenges simultaneously. The subscription model reduced piracy, lowered adoption barriers, and enabled faster innovation while creating more predictable revenue streams.

Looking forward, Adobe's journey offers enduring lessons about the importance of business model innovation in technology markets. The company's successful transition from perpetual licenses to subscriptions provides a template for other software companies considering similar transformations.

The success of Adobe's pivot also demonstrates how traditional software companies can reimagine their value proposition for the cloud era. While the fundamental value of Adobe's creative tools remained unchanged, the subscription model created new opportunities for innovation and market expansion.

Conclusion: Lessons from History's Greatest Business Transformations

Throughout this examination of remarkable corporate pivots, from Nintendo's evolution from playing cards to video games to Microsoft's transformation into a cloud computing leader, we have witnessed how successful companies can reinvent themselves in response to technological disruption, changing market conditions, and evolving customer needs. These transformations, while unique in their specific circumstances, reveal common patterns and principles that can guide business leaders facing similar challenges today.

The Anatomy of Successful Pivots

Successful business transformations consistently demonstrate several fundamental characteristics. First, they begin with clear-eyed recognition of existential threats or opportunities, often before these become obvious to the broader market. Fujifilm's early recognition of the digital photography threat and Netflix's anticipation of streaming video's potential exemplify this forward-looking perspective.

Second, successful pivots leverage core organizational capabilities in new ways. Nintendo applied its expertise in entertainment and gaming to video games, while Amazon transformed its internal technology infrastructure into AWS. These companies didn't abandon their fundamental strengths but rather found new applications for their core competencies.

Third, transformative success requires maintaining operational excellence during transition periods. Companies like Adobe and Microsoft successfully managed the delicate balance of sustaining existing revenue streams while building new business models. This dual capability—executing today while building for tomorrow—emerges as a crucial success factor.

The Role of Leadership

Leadership emerges as a critical factor in successful corporate transformations. Effective leaders demonstrate several key attributes:

The ability to articulate a compelling vision for transformation while acknowledging organizational heritage. Satya Nadella's leadership at Microsoft exemplifies this balance, respecting the company's past while charting a new direction.

The courage to make difficult decisions that may temporarily disadvantage existing business models. Netflix's decision to separate streaming from DVD rentals and Adobe's move to subscription pricing demonstrate this willingness to accept short-term disruption for long-term benefit.

The capacity to maintain organizational cohesion during periods of fundamental change. Fujifilm's ability to retain and retrain key technical talent while entering new markets illustrates this crucial leadership capability.

Strategic Implementation

Successful corporate pivots require careful attention to implementation strategy. The cases we've examined reveal several crucial principles:

Timing emerges as a critical factor. Companies that begin transformation while their core business remains strong—like Amazon and Microsoft—have more resources and strategic flexibility than those who wait until crisis forces change.

The importance of maintaining customer relationships during transformation cannot be overstated. Adobe's careful management of its transition to cloud subscriptions and IBM's focus on customer needs during its shift to services demonstrate how customer relationships can facilitate rather than impede transformation.

Investment in new capabilities must be balanced against maintaining existing operations. Marvel's methodical development of film production capabilities while maintaining its publishing business exemplifies this balanced approach to transformation.

Financial Considerations

Successful pivots require careful financial management. Leaders must balance the need for investment in new capabilities against maintaining current operations. This often involves:

Making significant upfront investments in new capabilities, as demonstrated by Microsoft's cloud infrastructure development and Netflix's investment in content production.

Managing investor expectations during transition periods, particularly when transformation involves short-term revenue or profit impacts, as seen in Adobe's shift to subscription pricing.

Maintaining sufficient financial flexibility to pursue opportunistic acquisitions or investments, as illustrated by Amazon's expansion into new markets and IBM's strategic acquisitions in consulting services.

Actionable Takeaways for Business Leaders

For contemporary business leaders contemplating or executing strategic transformations, several key lessons emerge:

Begin transformation before it becomes necessary. The most successful pivots start from positions of strength, not crisis. Regular assessment of market trends and potential disruptions should be institutionalized at the leadership level.

Identify and protect core capabilities while building new ones. Understanding what truly drives competitive advantage—often distinct from what drives current revenue—is crucial for successful transformation.

Invest in organizational culture and talent development. Successful transformations require both technical capabilities and adaptive organizational cultures that can embrace change while maintaining operational excellence.

Maintain close connection to customer needs and market evolution. Customer relationships and market understanding should guide transformation strategy, ensuring new directions align with evolving market requirements.

Looking Forward

As technological change continues to accelerate and industry boundaries become increasingly fluid, the ability to execute successful strategic pivots becomes ever more crucial for long-term corporate survival. The lessons from these historical transformations provide valuable guidance for leaders navigating contemporary challenges.

Yet each successful pivot also demonstrates the importance of context-specific adaptation. While the principles we've examined remain constant, their application must be tailored to specific organizational circumstances and market conditions.

The companies we've studied demonstrate that successful transformation is possible even in the face of dramatic technological and market changes. Their experiences offer both inspiration and practical guidance for business leaders tasked with similar challenges in an era of continuous disruption.

www.ingramcontent.com/pod-product-compliance
Lightning Source LLC
Chambersburg PA
CBHW070416230526
45471CB00006B/2839